The Trader's Mindset: 21 Rules to Master Your Psychology and Win in the Trading

How to Control Emotions, Build Discipline, and Achieve Long-Term Success

APURVA PARIKH

RAVI BHATT

PUBLISHED BY

APURVA PARIKH

(eapurva2000@gmail.com)

Copyright©2024 by Apurva S Parikh

Table of Contents

Dedication

To all the traders striving to master their mindset and emotions, this book is for you. May these 21 rules guide you to success, resilience, and clarity in your trading journey.

Acknowledgement

We express our deepest gratitude to our mentors, colleagues, and families for their unwavering support. Special thanks to all traders whose experiences inspired this book, shaping its lessons and insights.

Preface

Welcome to *The Trader's Mindset: 21 Rules to Master Your Psychology and Win in the Trading*! As you embark on this journey, remember that trading is more than just a numbers game; it's a complex dance with your own emotions and psychology. While many books focus solely on strategies, charts, and market trends, this book takes a different approach. It dives deep into the mindset that can either propel you to success or hold you back from achieving your trading goals.

In my 18 years of experience in the finance industry, I have witnessed numerous traders face challenges that stem not from a lack of knowledge, but from their inability to manage emotions. Fear, greed, overconfidence, and self-doubt can cloud judgment and lead to poor decisions. This is where mastering your psychology becomes essential. The truth is, that successful trading is not just about making the right moves in the market; it's about cultivating the right mindset.

In this book, you will discover 21 crucial rules that are designed to help you develop a resilient and disciplined mindset. Each rule is grounded in real-world experiences and is accompanied by practical strategies to help you overcome common psychological pitfalls. You will learn how to embrace uncertainty, respect risk instead of fearing it, and understand that losses are part of the game. By shifting your focus from chasing profits to mastering your emotions, you will cultivate a more sustainable approach to trading.

Each chapter includes real-life stories and examples (only the name is changed due to privacy issues) that illustrate the power of a positive trading mindset. You will read about traders like yourself who faced challenges and ultimately triumphed by applying these principles. The actionable tips provided throughout the book are designed for immediate implementation, allowing you to see tangible improvements in your trading performance.

Whether you are just starting your trading journey or are a seasoned trader looking to refine your skills, this book is for you. By mastering your psychology, you can unlock your true potential and achieve greater financial success.

As you read through these pages, I encourage you to reflect on your mindset and consider how these rules can apply to your trading journey. Remember, the path to success begins in your mind, and with the right mindset, you can transform your trading experience for the better. Let's dive in and explore the powerful mindset needed to thrive in the world of trading!

About the author

Apurva Parikh

Mr. Apurva Parikh is the author of the Book and is a Finance and Stock Market Coach with over 18 years of experience in the finance industry. He has an Honorary Doctorate in Finance, an MBA in Finance, an LLB, and a CAIIB, showcasing his extensive knowledge and expertise. Mr. Apurva specializes in various financial areas including investment, wealth management, stock markets, banking, loans, and project funding. He runs a successful financial consultancy firm, helping individuals and businesses achieve their financial goals.

His book, "8 Financial Secrets for Entrepreneurs," has become a #1 International Best Seller in four categories, while "The 7 Secrets to Financial Freedom for Women" has also reached #1 Best Seller status on Amazon India. Apurva's interests span finance, sales and marketing, emotional intelligence, and spirituality, reflecting his holistic approach to financial and personal growth.

Books by Author

-https://www.amazon.in/Secrets-Financial-Freedom-Women-Protect-ebook/dp/B08JQQGRG5

https://www.amazon.in/Financial-Secrets-Entrepreneurs-Insiders-Enterprises-ebook/dp/B08NHN9WDN

https://www.amazon.in/Secrets-Improve-Your-CIBIL-Score-ebook/dp/B08YVQKT47

https://www.amazon.in/Financial-Mistakes-that-keep-poor-ebook/dp/B093FHKSFC

https://www.amazon.in/Secrets-find-Value-Stocks-Consistently-ebook/dp/B0BMLL4Q6Z

RAVI BHATT

Mr Ravi Bhatt, a distinguished SEBI registered research analyst and the visionary founder of Cap Savaj embodies a consummate financial analyst with a decade-long journey in the industry. His academic laurels include an MBA in Finance complemented by an esteemed FRM certification, underscoring his commitment to mastering the intricacies of the financial realm.

Words from Authors

Dear Readers,

Welcome to "The Trader's Mindset: 21 Rules to Master Your Psychology and Win in the Trading Game." We, Apurva Parikh and Ravi Bhatt, are excited to embark on this journey with you. As seasoned traders ourselves, we have experienced the highs and lows that the financial markets bring. Through our extensive experience in the trading world, we have come to understand that success in trading is not merely about numbers, strategies, or market analysis; it's profoundly tied to the mindset we cultivate.

Many aspiring traders dive headfirst into the markets, driven by the promise of quick profits. However, what often goes unnoticed is the critical role of psychology in shaping trading outcomes. Emotions like fear, greed, and impatience can cloud judgment and lead to poor decision-making. Our goal with this book is to illuminate these psychological pitfalls and arm you with practical rules to navigate them successfully.

In "The Trader's Mindset," we present 21 essential rules that serve as your roadmap to mastering the mental aspects of trading. Each rule is backed by real-life examples and insights from our journeys, helping you relate to the concepts on a personal level. Whether you're a novice or an experienced trader, these rules are designed to resonate with you and enhance your trading acumen.

We emphasize that trading is not just about executing orders; it's about developing a disciplined approach, managing risk, and most importantly, understanding yourself. The journey may not always be smooth, but the principles outlined in this book will guide you to stay resilient and focused on your goals.

As you read through each chapter, we encourage you to reflect on your own experiences, identify your strengths and weaknesses, and apply these rules to your trading practice. We believe that with the right mindset and tools, you can unlock your potential and achieve the success you aspire to in the markets.

Thank you for choosing to explore "The Trader's Mindset." We are thrilled to have you with us, and we hope this book becomes a valuable companion in your trading journey.

Happy trading!

Warm regards,

Apurva Parikh & **Ravi Bhatt**

Special Thanks

We extend our heartfelt gratitude to **Mr. Romil Shah (CFA)** and **Mr. Sankalp Chaturvedi** (SEBI Registered Research Analyst) for their invaluable guidance and insights throughout the writing of this book. Their expertise and thoughtful contributions have enriched the content and helped shape the concepts presented.

21 Chapters- 21 Rules

1. Master Your Emotions, Master Your Trades

In stock market trading, the two most powerful emotions are fear and greed. These emotions can drive us to make bad decisions. Fear makes us sell too early, worried that the market will crash, and greed makes us hold on for too long, hoping for more profit even when it's time to exit. Both these emotions cloud our judgment, and once we lose control over them, they control us.

A Successful trader must learn to control their emotions and not let them dictate their trading decisions. When you master your emotions, you make decisions based on logic and strategy, not on panic or excitement. For example, when a stock is falling, a trader driven by fear might sell in a hurry, locking in a loss. But a calm and disciplined trader might recognize that the drop is temporary, based on market noise, and hold onto the stock or even buy more at a lower price. Similarly, when a stock is rising, a greedy trader might hold on longer than they should, expecting bigger profits, and then end up losing when the price eventually falls.

The stock market itself is neutral; it doesn't care about your feelings or what you want. It moves based on demand, supply, and economic factors. The best way to respond to the market is with the same neutrality. It's important to remain detached from the highs and lows. A rising stock price shouldn't make you euphoric, and a falling price shouldn't make you panic.

In practical terms, mastering your emotions means having a plan before you make any trade. You should know at what price you will enter a trade, where you will set your stop-loss, and what your exit strategy is for taking profits. Once you have a plan, stick to it, no matter what your emotions tell you during the trade. For instance, if you set a stop-loss and the stock is falling, you shouldn't hesitate to sell just because you hope it will go back up. Likewise, if the stock is rising and you've hit your target, take the profit and exit, instead of getting greedy and hoping for more.

One way to manage emotions is to keep a trading journal. Write down why you made each trade, what your emotions were, and whether or not you followed your plan. Over time, you'll see patterns in your emotional behaviour and can work on controlling them. **Another technique is to take breaks from the screen.** Constantly watching price movements can stir up emotions. Walking away or taking a break helps clear your mind.

In the end, the best traders are those who can control their emotions. They don't let fear or greed take over. They make decisions based on data, analysis, and strategy. When you master your emotions, you gain control over your trading, and that's when you truly start to win in the market.

Example :

In trading, emotions can cloud our judgment, leading to decisions that cost us dearly. Let me tell you about my friend Rajesh. He started trading in 2010 and now lives in the USA. Back when he was in India, Rajesh worked for Company X for eight years—it was his first and only job in India. Despite moving on from the company, he remains deeply attached to it.

Company X has been struggling over the past three years—sales have dropped, institutional investors are pulling out, and its market share is shrinking. Yet, Rajesh keeps buying its stock. Why? Because he's emotionally tied to the company. It's not about the numbers for him, it's about the memories. His time at Company X shaped him, so he holds onto the stock, hoping for a turnaround.

This is where emotions become dangerous. Rajesh is ignoring all the warning signs—decreasing profits, investor exits—because his heart refuses to let go. But in trading, emotions like these can kill profits. Rational decision-makers focus on facts, not feelings, and they often end up making better choices.

2. <u>Detach from the Outcome</u>

As a trader, it's easy to get caught up in the results. After all, we trade to make profits, and the excitement of seeing profits pile up can drive us to focus too much on the result. But the problem with this is that when you obsess over profits, you start making poor decisions. Instead of focusing on executing your strategy, you might chase profits, take unnecessary risks, or panic when things don't go as planned.

In trading, discipline is everything. **When you detach yourself from the outcome, you're able to follow your strategy without getting distracted by temporary gains or losses. The goal is not to make every single trade a winner but to follow a consistent process that makes you profitable over time.** If you're only thinking about the money, you might lose sight of what matters—making good trades, one at a time.

It's important to understand that no strategy will guarantee success in every trade. Sometimes, even if you do everything right, the market will go against you. But that doesn't mean your strategy was wrong. **A good trader knows that losses are part of the game and focuses on the long-term picture**. By sticking to your plan and detaching from individual outcomes, you increase your chances of success over time.

Another way to practice detachment is to think of yourself as an operator, not an owner. Your job is to execute the system, just like a machine follows a programmed set of instructions. Whether the trade is successful or not is secondary. This mental approach helps to reduce emotional stress and prevents you from reacting impulsively to market movements. For example, if your system tells you to enter a trade at a certain price and exit at another, you should do that without hesitation, even if the market looks uncertain at the moment.

Finally, detachment helps to maintain balance in your life. Trading can be stressful, especially when you're emotionally invested in the outcomes. But if you focus on the process rather than the results, you'll find that your stress levels go down. You'll trade with a clearer mind, make fewer emotional decisions, and find yourself in a better position to succeed in the long run.

By practising detachment, you become a more disciplined, focused, and effective trader.

Example

In trading, one of the hardest lessons to learn is to detach from the outcome. Let me introduce you to Sunil, a trader who's been in the stock market for five years. Last year, he invested heavily in a promising tech company. The company had strong earnings and good growth prospects, and everything seemed perfect. Sunil was confident this trade would make him a fortune.

As the stock price rose, so did his excitement. He began to imagine all the things he could do with his profits—a new house, a luxury car, and even an early retirement. But then, suddenly, the market turned. A bad earnings report sent the stock price tumbling. Sunil panicked. He wasn't prepared for this. He had become so attached to the idea of winning big that when things didn't go as planned, he couldn't handle the emotional hit. He sold in a rush, locking in heavy losses.

The problem wasn't just the market. Sunil had tied his happiness to the outcome of one trade. In trading, it's crucial to stay detached from results—win or lose. It's not about one trade, but about managing your mindset and sticking to your strategy over the long term.

3. <u>Respect Risk, Don't Fear It</u>

In the stock market, every trade carries some level of risk. You cannot avoid it, but you can manage it. Many new traders get scared when they think about risk. They fear losing money, and this fear often stops them from making decisions or pushes them into making bad ones. But the key to success in trading is not to avoid risk—it's about respecting it.

To respect risk means understanding that it's a natural part of trading and then planning how to handle it. **This is where tools like stop-loss orders and position sizing come into play**. A stop-loss is a price point where you decide to sell a stock to prevent further loss. For example, if you buy a stock at ₹100 and set a stop-loss at ₹90, it means that if the stock price falls to ₹90, you will sell automatically. This limits your loss to ₹10 per share. By using a stop-loss, you can limit your downside and keep your emotions in check, as you know exactly how much you're willing to lose.

Position sizing is another important aspect of risk management. It means deciding how much money to put into each trade. For example, instead of putting all your money into one stock, you can divide it among several stocks. This way, even if one trade goes wrong, your overall loss is smaller. A good rule is to never risk more than 1-2% of your total capital on a single trade. This keeps your losses manageable and helps you stay in the game longer.

When you respect risk, you also create a trading plan. A trading plan is a set of rules you follow for each trade. It includes your entry point (when to buy), your stop-loss (when to sell if the trade goes against you), and your target price (when to sell if the trade goes in your favour). Having a plan helps you stay calm and make decisions based on logic rather than emotions like fear or greed.

The opposite of respecting risk is fearing it. Fear paralyzes you. It makes you hesitate when you should be acting. For example, you may see a good opportunity to buy a stock, but the fear of losing money may stop you from entering the trade. Or you may hold on to a losing trade, hoping it will turn around, because you are too scared to take the loss. In both cases, fear leads to bad decisions.

On the other hand, when you respect risk, you don't let fear control you. You understand that losing trades is a part of the process, and by managing risk, you can keep those losses small. The goal is not to avoid losing, but to make sure that when you do lose, it doesn't hurt you too much.

In conclusion, risk is a part of every trade, but it doesn't have to be something you fear. By using tools like stop-losses, position sizing, and a solid trading plan, you can respect risk and manage it effectively. This helps you stay calm, focused, and ready to take advantage of opportunities without being paralyzed by fear.

Examples

In trading, managing risk is crucial, but fearing it can lead to poor decisions. Take my friend Imran, for example. He's intelligent but struggles as a trader due to his poor stop-loss management. He often sets very tight stop-losses, driven by fear of losing too much. While it seems cautious, this strategy has hurt him more than helped.

In about 70% of his trades, Imran's stop-loss gets triggered, and he ends up booking losses. Ironically, after his stop-loss hits, the market often bounces back just as he expected, but by then, it's too late. His fear of losing causes him to cut trades too soon, missing potential gains.

The key lesson here is to respect risk, but not fear it. Tight stop-losses based on fear rather than strategy can sabotage your trades. Proper risk management allows you to stay in the game and benefit from your well-thought-out positions.

4. The Market is Always Right

One of the first lessons every trader learns is that the market is always right. This means that no matter what you think or feel, the market will do what it wants. **You cannot control the market, and if you try to fight it, you will lose.** The market doesn't care about your opinion or predictions—it moves based on a complex mix of factors like demand, supply, and economic events.

Many traders, especially beginners, make the mistake of thinking they can outsmart the market. They may have done a lot of research and feel very confident about a trade. But sometimes, no matter how much research you do, the market may not move in the direction you expected. For example, you might be sure that a particular stock will go up, but instead, it starts falling. In this situation, some traders refuse to accept that they were wrong. They hold on to their losing position, hoping the market will change and prove them right. But often, this only leads to bigger losses.

Accepting that the market is always right means accepting when you are wrong. If a trade is not going as planned, it's important to cut your losses and move on. There is no room for ego in trading. The moment you start fighting the market, you are on the path to losing more money. Instead, the smart thing to do is to adapt to what the market is showing you. If the trend is against you, it's better to exit the trade and reassess rather than wait for a miracle.

The market is driven by trends, and successful traders learn to go with these trends rather than against them. For example, if the market is in a strong uptrend, it's usually a good idea to follow the trend and buy stocks that are rising. On the other hand, if the market is in a downtrend, it might be better to avoid buying stocks and wait for a better opportunity. Trying to predict when the market will reverse is risky and often leads to losses.

It's also important to remember that the market doesn't owe you anything. Just because you made money on one trade doesn't mean the market will continue to reward you. Similarly, just because you lost money on a trade doesn't mean the market is against you. The market is neutral; it moves based on its logic, and it's up to you to adjust your strategies accordingly.

In India, we have a saying: "Jo dikhta hai, wahi bikta hai," which means "What is visible, is what sells." This is true in the stock market as well. Trade is based on what you see, not what you hope for. The market will always tell you where it's headed—you just have to listen. Follow the signals, respect the trends, and don't try to impose your will on the market.

In summary, the market is always right because it represents the collective actions of all traders and investors. Accept this fact, and don't fight it. By going with the flow of the market and adapting to its movements, you put yourself in a much stronger position to succeed.

Example

In trading, the market has a way of humbling even the most experienced traders. Let me tell you about Kunal, a trader who loves to trade during major events. On 24th February 2022, when the Russia-Ukraine war broke out, Kunal saw an opportunity. Based on both technical and fundamental analysis, he aggressively shorted the market, expecting it to crash further due to the uncertainty and fear.

By the end of the day, he was sitting on solid profits, and the market looked scary enough to justify holding onto his positions. Kunal thought, "The market will fall more tomorrow." Confident in his analysis, he decided to keep all his positions open overnight.

But the next day, on 25th February 2022, the market surprised everyone. Instead of continuing to fall, it rallied, with the Nifty jumping up by almost 2.5%. Kunal's profits vanished, and he ended up booking a loss. The market had completely ignored the negative fundamentals he was so focused on.

This is the hard truth: the market is always right, no matter how strong your analysis may seem. It's not about what should happen, it's about what is happening. Traders must respect the market, not fight it.

5. <u>Overtrading is Emotional Trading</u>

Overtrading happens when a trader places too many trades without proper reason. Many times, this happens because of emotions like impatience, excitement, or even boredom. For example, you may feel like you're missing out on market action, or you may want to make quick money, so you keep entering and exiting trades without any proper analysis or strategy. This is not only risky but also a sure way to lose money.

In the stock market, patience is as important as knowledge. The urge to constantly buy and sell stocks often stems from the idea that you must always be doing something to make profits. However, this is not true. Some of the most successful traders make fewer trades but only when they see a high-probability setup. This means they wait for the right opportunity, and when it comes, they make their move. For example, a good trader will wait for the stock to reach a certain price level or show a specific pattern before buying. If none of these conditions are met, they simply do nothing.

Overtrading is closely linked to emotional trading because it shows that the trader is not in control of their emotions. Instead of following a plan, they are reacting to their feelings. This leads to poor decisions. For example, after a few losses, a trader may feel frustrated and enter another trade just to "win back" their money. This kind of behaviour often leads to bigger losses because the trade is made out of emotion, not logic or analysis.

The right way to approach trading is to treat it like a business. Every trade should have a reason behind it, backed by research and a clear plan. Ask yourself, "Why am I entering this trade?" If the answer is based on emotions like excitement or fear of missing out (FOMO), it's a sign that you're overtrading. **A disciplined trader waits for clear signals before taking action**. This might mean sitting out during certain market conditions, even if it feels boring.

One strategy to avoid overtrading is to create a trading plan and stick to it. Set clear rules for when to enter and exit trades, and follow these rules no matter how the market moves. Also, it's important to take breaks. Staring at the screen all day can create anxiety and make you feel like you need to act. Sometimes, stepping away from the computer and coming back with a fresh mind helps you stay disciplined.

In conclusion, overtrading is driven by emotions and is a quick way to lose money. Instead, focus on making fewer, high-quality trades based on proper analysis and strategy. The stock market rewards patience, not constant action. **For example, I take a maximum of two trades a day, if there is profit in one trade, I don't take another and when there is loss I take another trade. But if there is a loss in another, I stop trading on that day. So maximum of two trades a day.**

Example

Overtrading is like slow poison for traders. Let me tell you about Pranav, an options scalper who fell victim to overtrading. He trades options every day and follows a low stop-loss strategy, setting just 0.5% of his total capital as a stop-loss. On average, he makes 10 to 15 trades daily, believing that small, frequent trades will minimize his risk.

However, despite his low stop-loss theory, Pranav lost 55% of his capital last month. Why? Because on loss-making days, his emotions took over. Instead of accepting the loss, he kept trading more, trying to recover. On good days, he made profits, but on bad days, he overtraded, letting his frustration drive his decisions.

This shows how overtrading often stems from emotional reactions, especially when losses occur. It's not about the strategy alone—controlling emotions and avoiding excessive trading is crucial for long-term success.

6. <u>**Consistency Beats Perfection**</u>

In trading, many people try to make the "perfect" trade—one that buys at the lowest point and sells at the highest. However, the reality is that perfect trades are almost impossible to achieve consistently. The market is unpredictable, and trying to time everything perfectly can lead to stress, over-analysis, and missed opportunities. **Instead, what matters most in the long run is consistency.**

Consistency means sticking to a proven strategy and following it, trade after trade. **It's about doing the right things repeatedly, even if each trade is not perfect**. For example, a trader who consistently follows a set of rules—like buying only when a stock hits a specific support level and selling when it reaches a resistance level—will likely make money over time, even if they miss some perfect entry or exit points.

On the other hand, chasing perfection often leads to analysis paralysis. Traders who are obsessed with perfection tend to overanalyze every little detail, trying to find the exact right moment to buy or sell. They may hesitate to pull the trigger, fearing that they haven't found the perfect trade. This often leads to missed opportunities or, worse, losses because they waited too long.

In trading, it's better to have a strategy that works 60-70% of the time but is applied consistently than to try to find the "perfect" trade every time. For example, a trader may have a strategy that makes small but consistent profits on most trades, and sometimes they may have losses. Over time, these consistent wins will add up, and the occasional loss won't hurt much.

A great example of this is the story of long-term investors like Warren Buffett. Buffett doesn't aim to buy stocks at the lowest possible price or sell them at the peak. Instead, he focuses on finding good companies and holding them for the long term, trusting that their value will grow over time. His consistency in following this approach has made him one of the most successful investors in the world.

To build consistency in trading, it's important to create a set of rules or a trading plan and stick to it. This includes setting clear entry and exit points, managing risk, and controlling emotions. Once you have a plan, don't change it just because of one bad trade or one missed opportunity. Over time, following a consistent strategy will lead to better results than constantly changing your approach in search of perfection.

In summary, perfection in trading is an illusion. Instead, aim for consistency. A trader who follows a well-thought-out plan regularly will perform better over time than someone who is always searching for the perfect trade.

Example:

Most traders face losses in the stock market due to a lack of consistency. Let me tell you about Arjun, a trader who has achieved over 70% consistency in the derivatives market. What sets him apart from others is his dedication to research and preparation. Arjun has built his research setup, using data from the last 15 years and leveraging AI tools to refine his strategies.

Before entering any trade, he runs it through his system. Only if his system gives the green light does he take the trade. This disciplined approach ensures that his decisions are not driven by impulse or emotions but by solid analysis.

Arjun's success shows that consistency in trading isn't just about luck—it requires a strong, personal research setup. When you master your emotions and rely on a well-tested system, you can achieve consistency and success in your trades.

7. <u>Losses Are Part of the Game</u>

One of the most important lessons in trading is understanding that losses are inevitable. No matter how experienced or skilled a trader is, there will always be trades that don't go as planned. **The key to long-term success is not avoiding losses but learning how to deal with them**.

Many traders, especially beginners, fear losses. This fear can lead to hesitation, avoiding trades, or even worse—holding onto losing trades in the hope that they will turn around. But the truth is, every successful trader has faced losses. **The difference between successful traders and those who fail is how they manage those losses.**

Embracing losses as part of the game means accepting that not every trade will be a winner. Instead of seeing a loss as a failure, see it as a learning opportunity. For example, after a losing trade, a good trader will go back and analyze what went wrong. Was it a bad entry point? Did they fail to set a stop-loss? Was the market trend misjudged? By analyzing their mistakes, traders can improve and avoid repeating the same errors.

Another important aspect of managing losses is setting stop-losses. A stop-loss is a predetermined point where you will exit a trade to prevent further loss. For example, if you buy a stock at ₹500 and set a stop-loss at ₹450, it means that if the stock price falls to ₹450, you will sell automatically, limiting your loss to ₹50 per share. Using stop-losses is a simple but powerful way to manage losses and protect your capital.

One of the worst mistakes traders make is holding onto losing positions, hoping that the market will turn in their favour. This is called "hope trading," and it often leads to even bigger losses. Instead of hoping, it's better to cut your losses early and move on. Successful traders know that taking a small loss is much better than letting a small loss turn into a big one.

In conclusion, losses are a natural part of trading. Rather than fearing them, traders should accept losses as a learning experience and use tools like stop-losses to manage them. By treating losses as part of the journey, traders can stay focused, improve over time, and ultimately succeed in the stock market.

Example –

In trading, losses are inevitable, and understanding this is crucial. Take the example of Reliance Power in 2008. The stock launched with an issue price of ₹280, and there was a frenzy in the market, with many expecting huge returns. The public issue was oversubscribed, and optimism ran high.

However, soon after listing, the stock started to fall. At first, the losses were small—manageable and a signal to exit. But many investors, driven by hope, continued to hold onto their shares, convinced that a turnaround would come. Unfortunately, it never did. By 2020, the stock had plummeted to just ₹1, wiping out nearly the entire investment.

This story shows that losses are part of the game. The key is not to hold onto hope blindly. Recognizing when to cut losses and move on is an important lesson in trading psychology.

8. <u>Trust Your System</u>

In trading, having a reliable system or strategy is crucial, but what's equally important is trusting that system once you've put it into action. Many traders, especially beginners, tend to doubt their strategies when things don't go as expected mid-trade. They may enter a trade based on a plan, but as soon as the market moves against them, they start second-guessing their decisions. This can lead to emotional reactions like panic-selling, which often results in unnecessary losses.

Imagine you've done thorough research, set up a solid trading system, and entered a trade. However, the stock price doesn't move in the direction you predicted right away. At this point, fear and doubt may creep in, making you question your system. You might feel the urge to close the trade prematurely or make impulsive changes to your plan. This is where many traders go wrong—they let their emotions take control instead of sticking to their strategy.

Trusting your system means allowing it to play out, whether it leads to a win or a loss. Every system will have losing trades; no strategy can guarantee 100% success. The key is to follow your plan consistently over time. If your system has been tested and proven to work in the long run, it will recover from small losses and bring profits overall. But if you keep changing your approach based on short-term outcomes, you'll never know whether your strategy works.

A good way to build trust in your system is through backtesting. This means looking at how your strategy would have performed in past market conditions. By testing it over different periods and market scenarios, you can gain confidence that it will work in the future as well. Once you have this confidence, sticking to your system becomes much easier.

Another way to avoid doubting your strategy is to set clear rules before entering a trade. These rules should cover when to enter, where to place a stop-loss, and when to exit for profit. Once the trade is live, your job is to follow these rules without letting emotions interfere. It's important to remember that the market can be unpredictable in the short term, but if your system is built on sound principles, it will perform well over time.

In conclusion, trusting your system is a vital part of successful trading. Doubts and emotions can cloud your judgment, leading to poor decisions. By sticking to your strategy, accepting both wins and losses and avoiding mid-trade second-guessing, you increase your chances of long-term success.

Example –

During the IT bull run of 2020-2021, HCL Tech's share price skyrocketed from ₹500 to ₹1250. Many investors, seeing the strong momentum, entered at ₹1250 in January 2022, expecting further gains. But soon after, rising inflation in the USA led to an increase in interest rates by the Federal Reserve, causing the stock price to decline to around ₹850.

Despite the drop, HCL Tech's financials remained solid, showing only a marginal decline in performance. Some panicked and sold their shares at a loss, but those who trusted their system and believed in the company's fundamentals held on. Now, with inflation under control, the stock has reached an all-time high of ₹1845 on 11th October 2024.

This example shows the importance of trusting your system. Market fluctuations are inevitable, but if your analysis and strategy are sound, patience can often lead to rewarding outcomes in the long run.

9. <u>Patience Pays More Than Speed</u>

In the world of stock trading, many people believe that quick decisions lead to quick profits. While it's true that sometimes the market moves fast, the best trades often require a lot of patience. **Rushing into a trade without waiting for the right setup can lead to impulsive decisions, which may result in losses.**

Patience in trading means waiting for the perfect opportunity to enter the market. It could be days or even weeks before a stock shows the right pattern or price level that matches your strategy. However, many traders, especially those who are new or excited, feel the need to act quickly. They may jump into a trade without proper analysis, driven by emotions like excitement or fear of missing out (FOMO). This often leads to poor results because the trade wasn't backed by a solid plan.

Think of trading like fishing. A good fisherman doesn't cast his net every few minutes hoping to catch fish. He waits patiently until he sees the right conditions. Similarly, in trading, acting too fast can cause you to make impulsive decisions, while waiting for the best setup often leads to better results. For example, a stock might be moving up, but it hasn't yet reached a level where it's safe to buy. If you act too quickly, you might buy at a high price and then watch the stock fall, resulting in a loss.

Another important aspect of patience is waiting for trades to develop after you've entered them. Some traders expect instant results and get frustrated if the market doesn't immediately move in their favour. This frustration can cause them to exit trades too early, missing out on potential profits. However, if you have a solid plan and are patient, the market may eventually move in the direction you anticipated, giving you the gains you were aiming for.

Patience is not just about waiting to enter or exit trades—it's also about understanding that trading is a long-term game. The goal is not to make a quick profit today but to build consistent wealth over time. By rushing, you may make quick money once or twice, but consistent profits come from a disciplined, patient approach.

In conclusion, patience is a key trait that separates successful traders from those who struggle. By waiting for the right setup, avoiding impulsive actions, and allowing your trades to develop, you position yourself for better results in the long run. Remember, slow and steady wins the race.

Example –

There are many examples where patience in the stock market has led to significant wealth creation. Let me tell you about Rohit, who invested in Maruti Suzuki back in 2004 when it was listed at an issue price of ₹190. Over the years, the company rewarded its shareholders with bonuses and stock splits, and Rohit patiently held onto his shares, ignoring short-term market fluctuations.

Fast forward to 2024, and the stock is now trading at over ₹12,000. Considering the bonuses, dividends, and stock splits along the way, the stock has provided a massive 100x return over 20 years. This is a perfect example of how patience in the stock market can outperform any short-term gains.

10. <u>Cut Your Losses, Let Winners Run</u>

One of the most common mistakes traders make is holding onto losing trades, hoping that the market will turn around and they will recover their losses. This is a psychological trap known as "hope trading." Instead of accepting the loss and moving on, many traders hang onto their losing positions, watching the stock fall further and further. On the other hand, **some traders also make the mistake of selling winning trades too early, out of fear that the price might drop**. Both these behaviours can hurt your overall performance in the stock market.

The phrase **"Cut your losses, let your winners run" is a golden rule in trading**. It means that you should accept small losses when the market goes against you, but when the market moves in your favour, you should allow the trade to continue making profits. In simple terms, you should limit your losses and maximize your gains.

Let's start with cutting losses. Every trader should have a clear plan before entering a trade, which includes a stop-loss. A stop-loss is a predetermined point at which you will exit the trade if it goes against you. For example, if you buy a stock at ₹500, you might set a stop-loss at ₹450. If the stock drops to ₹450, you will sell automatically, limiting your loss to ₹50 per share. This way, you avoid large losses, which can wipe out your capital. Many traders, however, avoid using stop-losses or remove them once the trade starts losing money, hoping that the stock will bounce back. This is a dangerous approach, as it can lead to much larger losses.

On the other hand, letting winners run means allowing profitable trades to continue growing. When a stock moves in your favour, resist the urge to sell too early just because you've made some profit. Instead, allow the stock to keep moving in the positive direction as long as the market shows strength. For example, if you buy a stock at ₹500 and it rises to ₹600, you might be tempted to sell and take the profit. However, if the market trend is still strong, you could continue holding the stock, potentially making even more profit.

One of the best ways to manage this is to use trailing stop-losses. A trailing stop moves your stop-loss up as the stock price rises, protecting your profits while allowing the trade to continue running. For example, if the stock rises from ₹500 to ₹600, you can move your stop-loss up to ₹550. This way, if the stock drops, you will still exit with a profit.

In conclusion, the key to success in trading is to cut your losses quickly and let your profitable trades continue to grow. By following this rule, you can protect your capital and maximize your gains, leading to more consistent profits over time.

Example

In trading, knowing when to cut your losses is just as important as letting your winners run. Take the case of Neha, who invested in Dredging Corporation stock during its stellar run in the first half of 2024. The stock price soared from ₹650 to ₹1468, and analysts were optimistic, predicting it would reach ₹2,400 by year-end. Neha bought in at ₹1450, excited by the potential.

However, when the company's Q1 2024 financial results disappointed, it was a clear signal to set a stop-loss to protect her investment. Instead of doing so, she held on, hoping for a turnaround. The stock fell to ₹1,250 and remained around that level in July. Without a trailing stop-loss, Neha faced further pain as institutional sell-offs dragged the stock down to ₹850 by August.

Neha's experience highlights a crucial lesson: cutting losses early can save your capital for better opportunities down the road.

11. <u>Trade What You See, Not What You Feel</u>

In the stock market, emotions can be a trader's worst enemy. **Often, traders make decisions based on their feelings rather than relying on data, charts, and facts. This leads to poor decisions, impulsive trades, and ultimately, losses**. The rule "Trade What You See, Not What You Feel" is a simple yet powerful reminder to focus on hard evidence instead of letting emotions drive your actions.

Imagine this: You have a feeling that a particular stock is going to go up because you read some positive news about the company. You feel excited and decide to buy the stock, even though the technical signals—like price patterns or indicators—are not showing any signs of an upward movement. You're relying on your gut feeling rather than what the charts and data are telling you. The stock might go up based on luck, but more often than not, you'll find that emotional trading leads to disappointment.

In trading, it's essential to separate facts from feelings. Emotions like fear, greed, excitement, and frustration can cloud your judgment. For example, if a trader sees the market moving up rapidly, they might feel FOMO (Fear of Missing Out) and jump into a trade without proper analysis. On the flip side, when the market starts to fall, fear might make them sell too soon, even if the stock is still fundamentally strong.

"Trading what you see" means focusing on objective data, such as price charts, technical indicators, and news that directly impacts stock prices. **A good trader will use tools like moving averages, support and resistance levels, and volume trends to make decisions.** These tools are based on market realities, not emotions. For instance, if a stock is consistently bouncing off a certain price level (support), this is a signal to buy rather than going by a gut feeling.

Another important aspect is sticking to your trading plan. A well-defined plan includes your entry and exit points, risk management strategies, and clear rules for when to buy and sell. When emotions start to creep in—whether it's excitement or fear—**it's important to stick to your plan instead of making impulsive decisions**. For example, if your plan says you will exit a trade when it reaches a specific stop-loss, don't let hope or fear make you hold onto the stock longer, hoping it will turn around.

One way to avoid emotional trading is by practising discipline. Discipline comes from consistently applying your strategy, regardless of how you feel in the moment. Many professional traders keep a trading journal to track their trades and review them later. This helps them stay objective and spot emotional trading habits. By reviewing their past trades, they can learn from their mistakes and improve over time.

In conclusion, trading based on emotions can lead to poor decisions and losses. It's important to focus on what the data and charts are telling you and to stick to your trading strategy. By separating your feelings from your decisions, you increase your chances of making successful trades.

Example

In trading, it's essential to focus on the market's reality rather than your emotions. Let me share the story of Vikram, a successful trader in the derivatives market. He's known for his event-driven trades and is a staunch supporter of the BJP. As the election results approached, he felt confident that the BJP would cross 400 seats, driven by his emotional attachment to the party.

However, when he saw the early election results before the market opened, he quickly changed his mind. The data suggested that the BJP would struggle to even reach 300 seats. At around 9:20 AM, Vikram acted on what he saw rather than what he felt. He bought MIDCAP Nifty Put options at a strike price of 11,600 for ₹270 and sold them later at ₹820.

This savvy decision earned him a 3x return in just one day. Vikram's experience perfectly illustrates the principle of trading what you see, not what you feel. If he had acted on his emotions, he would have faced losses instead.

12. <u>Separate Ego from Trading</u>

In the world of trading, the desire to be "right" can be dangerous. Many traders, especially beginners, enter the market with the mindset that they must win every trade to prove themselves. They become attached to their trades, seeing a loss as a personal failure or a sign that they were wrong. This attachment is driven by ego, which can cloud judgment and lead to costly mistakes.

The reality is, no trader is right all the time. Even the most successful traders have lost trades. Losses are a natural part of the process. The key is to understand that trading is not about being right; it's about making money. You can be wrong about a stock's movement and still make money if you manage your risks properly. Conversely, you can be right about a stock but lose money if you don't manage your trades well.

Ego-driven trading often leads to holding onto losing trades for too long. For example, if you enter a trade expecting the stock to rise, but it starts falling instead, your ego might prevent you from selling. You tell yourself, "I'm sure it will turn around," because admitting that the trade was a mistake feels like a blow to your self-esteem. This is how small losses turn into big losses.

On the other hand, traders who separate their ego from trading focus on the process, not the outcome. They understand that a single trade doesn't define their skills or worth as a trader. If a trade goes against them, they simply exit and move on to the next opportunity. There's no emotional attachment, and they don't see a loss as a personal failure. Instead, they view it as part of the game.

A good trader understands that the market is unpredictable. It's not a place where you can always be right, but it's a place where you can consistently make money if you manage your trades well. This is why **successful traders focus on risk management, not on being right all the time**. They know that the goal is to make more money on their winning trades than they lose on their losing trades.

One way to separate ego from trading is to adopt a mindset of humility and learning. **Instead of focusing on being right, focus on improving your trading skills**. Each trade, whether it's a win or a loss, offers valuable lessons. By staying humble and open to learning, you can continuously improve as a trader.

In conclusion, ego has no place in trading. The desire to be right can cloud your judgment and lead to poor decisions. Instead, focus on the process of making smart, disciplined trades. In the end, it's not about being right—it's about making money consistently.

Example –

In trading, it's vital to separate your ego from your decisions. Many Gujarati traders have a deep affection for Reliance Industries, often considering it a favourite stock. Over the years, Reliance has delivered solid returns, but in 2024, it has struggled to outperform the index. The stock has fluctuated between ₹2,600 and ₹3,200, providing only a 5% return while the Nifty has risen by 10%.

Despite this, many traders hold onto their Reliance shares, driven by emotional attachment rather than rational analysis. They ignore the fact that the stock is stuck in a range and fail to recognize when it's time to pivot.

To achieve better returns, it's crucial to let go of personal feelings and accept the reality of the market. By detaching your ego from trading decisions, you can make more objective choices and seize opportunities that lead to greater financial success.

13. <u>Stay Humble or Be Humbled</u>

The stock market is a place where anything can happen, and no trader, no matter how experienced, can predict the market with absolute certainty. Overconfidence is one of the biggest dangers in trading, and it often leads to large mistakes. The phrase **"Stay humble or be humbled" serves as a reminder that the market has the power to teach even the most successful traders a lesson if they become too confident.**

When a trader experiences a series of successful trades, it's easy to start feeling invincible. You might think you've figured out the market and that your strategy is foolproof. This overconfidence can lead to taking on bigger risks, ignoring proper risk management, or making impulsive decisions. For example, after a few wins, you might start trading larger positions without adjusting your risk, thinking that you're on a winning streak and nothing can go wrong.

However, the market is unpredictable, and the moment you think you've mastered it, it can surprise you with a big loss. Overconfidence leads to complacency, and complacency leads to mistakes. For instance, a trader who becomes overconfident might skip doing proper analysis before entering a trade or may ignore warning signals because they believe they're always right.

On the other hand, traders who remain humble understand that the market is always changing. They don't get carried away by a few wins, and they don't let losses crush their confidence. They stay grounded, knowing that success in trading comes from consistency, discipline, and continuous learning. These traders are always cautious, always respecting the market, and always aware that a single trade can wipe out their gains if they're not careful.

Staying humble also means being open to learning from others. The market is vast, and there's always something new to learn. **Humble traders seek advice, stay updated on market trends, and constantly refine their strategies.** They don't let their ego get in the way of learning, even if they've been successful in the past.

In conclusion, staying humble in the stock market is essential for long-term success. The moment you become overconfident, the market will remind you of its unpredictability. By staying grounded, respecting the market, and continuously learning, you can avoid costly mistakes and maintain consistent profits over time.

Example –

In trading, staying humble is essential, as the market has a way of keeping you grounded. Let's consider the story of Anil, an ambitious trader who had great success in 2023. During that year, he invested heavily in the real estate and defence sectors, which delivered spectacular returns. Riding high on his success, Anil became overconfident, believing he could predict the next big trend.

However, in 2024, the market shifted, and the Gems and Jewellery theme emerged as the new multi-bagger. While other traders adapted, Anil held onto his previous winners, convinced that they would continue to perform. As a result, he missed out on lucrative opportunities.

Anil's experience is a perfect reminder that the market is always evolving. Staying humble and being open to new themes can prevent traders from becoming complacent. In trading, it's not just about past successes; it's about continuously adapting to the ever-changing landscape.

14. <u>Focus on the Process, Not the Profits</u>

In the stock market, many new traders tend to fixate on making quick profits. Their primary goal is to earn money as fast as possible, often ignoring the importance of a solid trading process. However, seasoned traders understand that profits are simply a byproduct of a good trading process. **The key to long-term success in trading is to focus on improving your strategy and sticking to your plan, rather than obsessing over how much money you can make in a single trade.**

Let's break this down with an example. **Imagine a cricketer who only thinks about hitting sixes in every game. If they swing their bat wildly without focusing on technique, they might hit a few sixes in the beginning, but eventually, they'll lose their wicket because they aren't following a consistent process.** Similarly, in trading, if you focus only on making money without following a disciplined approach, you may have a few wins, but it won't last in the long run.

The process of trading involves many factors like analyzing the market, identifying good entry and exit points, managing risk, and sticking to your trading plan. These are the things you should focus on rather than constantly thinking about how much money you're making or losing. If you concentrate on improving each of these aspects of your trading process, the profits will come naturally.

For example, let's say you have a strategy that involves buying stocks when they are near a support level and selling them near a resistance level. The key is to consistently follow this strategy, even if some trades don't work out as expected. Over time, you'll realize that by focusing on this disciplined approach, your overall success rate improves, leading to better profits.

One of the biggest problems with focusing solely on profits is that it can lead to emotional decision-making. If you're always thinking about how much money you need to make, you might start taking unnecessary risks or making impulsive trades. This can result in bigger losses. However, if you focus on following your process, you'll stay calm and make more rational decisions, even during market fluctuations.

In the long run, a strong process will help you maintain consistency. **Trading is not a get-rich-quick scheme. It's a skill that requires patience, discipline, and continuous learning. Successful traders always prioritize improving their processes over chasing profits.** They know that if they keep refining their strategy and staying disciplined, the profits will follow automatically.

In conclusion, profits are a natural outcome of a well-executed trading process. By focusing on improving your strategy, managing risk, and following your trading plan, you'll set yourself up for long-term success in the stock market. Instead of chasing quick gains, focus on the process, and the profits will come.

Example :

One of my friends, Thomas, is a dedicated trader who spent years developing a research system based on nearly

30 years of market data. He launched his system after the COVID-19 pandemic in 2020, right when the market was in a bullish phase. Initially, Thomas was optimistic, but he quickly realized that his returns were below the market average, leading to doubts about the effectiveness of his system.

Despite his scepticism, he chose to focus on the process of refining his system rather than chasing profits. He diligently analyzed each trade, making adjustments based on his findings. Over time, his patience paid off. By the end of the following year, Thomas's system generated an impressive 120% return in delivery-based trading.

Thomas's journey highlights the importance of focusing on the process instead of fixating on immediate profits. When you invest time and effort into developing a solid trading strategy, the results will follow in due course.

15. <u>Avoid Revenge Trading</u>

One of the most common mistakes traders make after a losing trade is something called "revenge trading." This happens when a trader tries to quickly "win back" the money they lost by entering a new trade without proper analysis or planning. It's driven by frustration and anger rather than logic and strategy. Unfortunately, revenge trading usually leads to even bigger losses because it is based on emotion, not reason.

Imagine a scenario where you've just lost a significant amount of money in a trade. Naturally, you feel upset, and your first instinct is to make up for that loss as soon as possible. Instead of calmly analyzing the market and finding a new, well-thought-out trade, you hastily jump into another trade. This time, your goal is not to follow a strategy but to "get your money back." You're trading out of anger or frustration, and more often than not, this leads to another loss.

The problem with revenge trading is that it throws all logic and planning out the window. When you're emotional, you're more likely to make bad decisions. You might take on too much risk, ignore warning signs in the market, or rush into trades without waiting for the right opportunity. All of this increases your chances of losing even more money.

To avoid revenge trading, the first step is to accept that losses are a natural part of trading. **No trader, no matter how experienced, can win all the time.** Instead of trying to win back what you lost right away, it's better to step back and give yourself time to cool down. This allows you to clear your mind and approach the market with a fresh perspective.

One helpful strategy is to take a break after a losing trade. This could mean stepping away from your trading desk for a few hours or even taking a day off. By giving yourself space, you can calm down and avoid making impulsive decisions. When you return, you'll be in a better mental state to make logical and well-planned trades.

Another important aspect of avoiding revenge trading is having a solid risk management plan in place. Before entering any trade, you should know how much you're willing to lose if the trade goes against you. This will help you keep your losses small and manageable. With a good risk management plan, a single losing trade won't feel like a disaster, so you'll be less likely to seek revenge through reckless trading.

In conclusion, revenge trading is a dangerous trap that many traders fall into after a loss. It's driven by emotion rather than logic, and it usually leads to more losses. The best way to avoid it is to stay calm, accept losses as part of the game, and take a break if needed. By sticking to your trading plan and focusing on long-term success, you'll avoid the pitfalls of emotional trading.

Example:

Revenge trading is a common pitfall that can devastate a trader's career. Let me share the story of my friend, Harvindersingh, who fell victim to this mindset during the crude oil futures trading crash in 2015. As crude oil prices plummeted, Harvindersingh stubbornly believed that the market would rebound, so he kept taking buy positions despite incurring losses.

Initially, his losses were manageable, but instead of cutting his losses, he aggressively increased his positions in an attempt to recover. He also engaged in averaging down, hoping for a turnaround. However, the market continued to decline, and by 2016, Harvindersingh had lost nearly all of his trading capital.

This experience serves as a harsh reminder that in derivative trading, it's crucial to follow the trend and avoid the temptation of revenge trading. By doing so, traders can protect their capital and make more rational decisions, ultimately leading to long-term success.

16. <u>Trade in Alignment with Your Lifestyle</u>

Not all traders are the same, and neither are their lifestyles. Some people have the time and energy to watch the stock market closely throughout the day, while others may have jobs, families, or other commitments that prevent them from monitoring trades continuously. That's why it's important to choose a trading style that fits your lifestyle. Forcing yourself into a high-frequency or day trading style when you can't dedicate enough time to it is a recipe for stress and poor performance.

Let's say you have a full-time job that requires you to be busy during market hours. In this case, trying to follow a day trading strategy, where you need to make quick decisions every few minutes, would be very challenging. You won't be able to monitor the market consistently, which increases your chances of missing important signals and making costly mistakes. **Instead, it would be better to adopt a longer-term trading style like swing trading or position trading, where you hold trades for days, weeks, or even months**. This way, you don't have to keep an eye on the market all day, and you can analyze your trades after work in your free time.

On the other hand, if you're someone who can dedicate several hours a day to trading, then a more active trading style like day trading or scalping might suit you. These styles require quick decision-making and constant monitoring of the market, but they can also offer more frequent trading opportunities.

The key is to be honest with yourself about how much time and energy you can realistically devote to trading. There's no right or wrong trading style, only what works best for your situation. Trying to force yourself into a trading style that doesn't align with your lifestyle will only lead to frustration and mistakes. For example, if you're constantly distracted by other responsibilities, you might miss important trade signals or make hasty decisions.

Another important aspect of trading in alignment with your lifestyle is setting realistic expectations. **If you can only trade part-time, don't expect to make the same profits as a full-time professional trader.** It's important to manage your expectations and focus on consistent progress rather than trying to match the returns of someone who trades for a living.

In conclusion, your trading style should fit your lifestyle and schedule. Don't try to force a high-frequency trading style if you can't monitor the market all day. Instead, choose a strategy that works with your time constraints and commitments. This will help you stay calm, make better decisions, and ultimately be more successful in the stock market.

Example :

After the 2020 COVID-19 lockdown, many working-class individuals, especially those in IT, started exploring stock market trading. However, I noticed that many of these full-time employees were suffering significant losses in the derivative market. This is primarily because derivative trading requires constant attention and quick decision-making. When they tried to balance their jobs and trading, they often ended up losing in both areas.

Let me share a recent example involving my friend, Kiran, who works in an IT firm while actively trading in the derivative market. On September 20, 2024, Kiran bought a Sensex 84,300 Call Option at ₹35, investing ₹3,50,000 for 1,000 lots (with a lot size of 10 units). Just as he placed his order, he received a call from his seniors and had to rush to the office. In his haste, he forgot to set his target and stop loss. When he returned just 10 minutes later, he discovered that the option premium had skyrocketed to ₹305. Unfortunately, by the time he checked, it was trading around ₹90.

This experience underscores the importance of trading in alignment with one's lifestyle. Balancing both can lead to missed opportunities and significant losses.

17. <u>Know When to Step Away</u>

In trading, one of the most important lessons you can learn is knowing when to step away from the market. While it might seem counterintuitive to not trade when you have opportunities, sometimes the best move you can make is to take no action at all. This is especially true when emotions are running high or the market is unclear. Stepping back from trading during these times can save you from making impulsive decisions that lead to unnecessary losses.

Imagine you're in a situation where the market is very volatile—prices are moving up and down rapidly, and you're unsure of which direction the market will take. Many traders, in such scenarios, feel pressured to act. They may think that if they don't enter a trade, they're missing out on potential profits. But what often happens is that traders make rash decisions when they're uncertain, leading to poorly timed trades and losses.

Stepping away from the market in such conditions is a sign of discipline, not weakness. It allows you to avoid making emotional decisions and gives you time to reflect on your strategy. The stock market will always be there, but your capital may not be if you keep making impulsive trades. There's no harm in sitting out for a day or two, especially if you feel that your judgment is clouded or that the market isn't giving you clear signals.

It's also important to step away when emotions like fear, greed, or frustration take control of your

decision-making. For example, after a big loss, you might feel the urge to immediately jump back in and recover your money—this is known as revenge trading. Similarly, after a series of wins, overconfidence might make you take on unnecessary risks. In both cases, stepping away allows you to regain emotional balance and clarity. **You can return to the market with a cool head and make decisions based on logic and analysis rather than emotions.**

Knowing when to step away doesn't mean you're giving up on trading. It simply means you're waiting for a better opportunity. The market is like a river—it's constantly flowing and changing. Just because you don't trade today doesn't mean there won't be good opportunities tomorrow. Patience is a crucial trait for successful traders. It's better to wait for a clear setup that aligns with your strategy than to jump into the market blindly because you feel the need to trade.

In conclusion, stepping away from the market is an important aspect of trading psychology. It shows that you understand the importance of emotional control and patience. Whether it's because the market is unclear or you're feeling overwhelmed, taking a break allows you to regroup, come back with a fresh perspective, and make better trading decisions in the future.

Examples :

Successful traders always follow discipline and implement proper risk management. They often stick to their trading setups. Let me share an example of my friend, Ramesh, a successful trader who has his system. In September 2022, he achieved an impressive 30% return in just one month, boasting an accuracy of nearly 90%.

However, things took a turn in November and December when his accuracy plummeted to just 10%. As a result, he lost all the gains he had made in September. Recognizing that his setup was not working as it should, Ramesh made a crucial decision: he stepped away from the market for three months.

When he returned to trading in April 2023, he was refreshed and ready. This time, he approached the market with renewed focus and discipline, which led him back to being a successful trader. Ramesh's story highlights the importance of knowing when to step away to reassess and regroup.

18. <u>Fear of Missing Out (FOMO) Kills Profits</u>

One of the most dangerous emotions in trading is FOMO—Fear of Missing Out. This happens when you see other traders or the market making big moves, and you feel pressured to jump in because you don't want to miss out on potential profits. FOMO often leads to poor trading decisions, like entering trades without proper analysis or exiting too early because you're afraid of losing your gains. In the long run, this can kill your profits and lead to losses.

Imagine this: You see a stock suddenly going up, and social media is buzzing about how much money people are making from it. Even though you didn't plan to trade that stock, the excitement makes you feel like you need to get in on the action before it's too late. You enter the trade without doing your usual analysis, and by the time you've bought the stock, it's already nearing its peak. The price starts to drop soon after, and now you're stuck in a bad position because you acted out of fear rather than logic.

This is how FOMO works. It tricks your brain into thinking that you're missing out on an opportunity, so you rush into trades without proper planning. The result? You end up buying at the top or selling at the bottom, which leads to poor entry and exit points. FOMO clouds your judgment, and instead of following your well-thought-out trading plan, you start chasing the market.

The best way to overcome FOMO is to stick to your plan, no matter what the market or other traders are doing. A solid trading plan is based on your research, risk tolerance, and strategy. When you follow your plan, you make decisions based on facts and analysis, not emotions. If a stock is moving rapidly and it doesn't fit your criteria, it's okay to let it go. There will always be another opportunity.

It's also important to remember that you don't need to catch every move in the market to be successful. Many traders get caught up in the idea that they need to be in every big trade to make money, but that's not true. What matters is that the trades you do enter are well-researched and fit within your strategy. Focusing on quality over quantity will help you avoid the pitfalls of FOMO.

In conclusion, FOMO is a dangerous emotion that can lead to poor trading decisions and hurt your profits. The key to overcoming it is to trust your plan and not be swayed by what others are doing. Stick to your strategy, and don't chase the market out of fear—you'll find that this leads to more consistent and profitable trading in the long run.

Example

Most retail investors and option buyers often fall victim to the fear of missing out (FOMO). We all know that implied volatilities are crucial in option buying, but this fear can cloud judgment. Let me share an example of my friend, Deepak, who experienced this firsthand.

In the first half of September, Deepak was cautious and opted for a wait-and-watch approach, feeling uncertain about the market. However, as September progressed and

Nifty was trading around 26,200, he began to feel he had missed a golden buying opportunity. In a rush to catch up, he started buying call options on various stocks without proper analysis.

Unfortunately, just as he entered the market, FII selling triggered a sharp decline, and Deepak faced significant losses. His story serves as a reminder that letting FOMO drive trading decisions can lead to missed opportunities and substantial losses instead of profits.

19. <u>Embrace Uncertainty</u>

In the stock market, there are no guarantees. No one, no matter how experienced or knowledgeable, can predict exactly what will happen next. This is because the market is influenced by countless factors, including economic conditions, investor sentiment, company news, and global events. The key to becoming a successful trader is to embrace this uncertainty rather than trying to fight it or predict the future with absolute certainty.

Many traders fall into the trap of believing they can predict the market's next move. They spend hours analyzing charts, reading news, and following trends, hoping to find the "perfect" trade. While analysis is important, it's also crucial to understand that the market can always move in unexpected ways. Trying to predict every move can lead to frustration, stress, and even overtrading as you constantly second-guess yourself.

Embracing uncertainty means accepting that there will always be an element of unpredictability in the market. **Instead of trying to control or predict it, focus on managing your risk and being adaptable. For example, instead of trying to predict whether a stock will go up or down, you can prepare for both scenarios by setting stop losses and having a clear exit plan**. This way, you protect yourself from large losses while remaining open to potential gains.

One of the best ways to embrace uncertainty is by having a strong risk management plan. You can't control the market, but you can control how much you're willing to lose on any given trade. By setting a maximum loss for each trade, you reduce the emotional pressure of trying to predict the future and instead focus on managing the present. If a trade goes against you, you simply exit and move on to the next opportunity.

Another important aspect of embracing uncertainty is staying flexible. The market is constantly changing, and strategies that work in one environment may not work in another. Successful traders are those who adapt to new market conditions rather than sticking rigidly to a single approach. For example, during periods of high volatility, you might need to adjust your trading style to account for quicker price movements. Being flexible allows you to navigate the market's uncertainty more effectively.

In conclusion, uncertainty is an inevitable part of the stock market. Trying to predict every move is not only impossible but also stressful. By accepting that the market is unpredictable focusing on managing your risk and staying adaptable, you'll become a more confident and successful trader. Embrace the unknown, and you'll be better prepared to navigate whatever the market throws your way.

Examples

Uncertainty is like a double-edged sword in the trading world. While some traders thrive during volatile markets, where both risk and reward are high, others may find themselves struggling due to poor risk management. Let me share an example of my friend, Rohit, who faced this dilemma.

Rohit was excited about the upcoming quarterly results, knowing that volatility in stock prices often presents unique opportunities. However, during this uncertain period, he decided to invest in a loss-making company, convinced that its share price would rise based on speculative trends. Despite analyst predictions that the stock would fall, Rohit's emotional decision led him to ignore crucial risk management strategies.

As a result, when the quarterly results were released, the stock price skyrocketed unexpectedly. Rohit had a moment of elation, but it was short-lived as the stock soon plummeted, causing him significant losses. This experience taught him that while embracing uncertainty can lead to opportunities, a rational approach and effective risk management are essential for long-term success in trading.

20. <u>Stop Seeking Validation</u>

In trading, it's easy to fall into the habit of seeking validation from others. This might be from fellow traders, online forums, or even friends and family who know little about the stock market. Many new traders feel the need for approval or reassurance before making a trade or after facing a loss. They might ask others, "What do you think of this trade?" or "Should I sell now?" But successful traders understand that trading is a personal journey, and you must learn to trust your analysis, instincts, and decisions. **Seeking validation from others can weaken your confidence and prevent you from growing as a trader.**

Let's start by understanding why traders seek validation. One common reason is insecurity, especially for beginners. When you're just starting, the stock market can feel overwhelming, and you may doubt your knowledge or strategy. This is completely normal. However, instead of relying on your research and learning from your experiences, you may turn to others for reassurance. While it's fine to ask for advice from mentors or experts, constantly relying on others means you're not building your decision-making skills.

Another reason traders seek validation is the fear of being wrong. No one likes to make mistakes, especially when money is on the line. When you ask for someone else's opinion on a trade, it's often because you're trying to avoid the discomfort of making a wrong decision. But the truth is, in trading, mistakes are inevitable. Every trader, even the most experienced ones, makes bad trades at some point. The important thing is to learn from these mistakes and keep improving. Seeking validation from others will not help you avoid mistakes—it will only delay your growth as a trader.

The problem with relying on external validation is that it can cloud your judgment. Imagine you've done your research and identified a good trading opportunity. You feel confident about the trade, but then you ask a friend for their opinion, and they discourage you from entering the trade. You end up listening to them and miss out on a profitable opportunity. Or worse, you enter a trade based on someone else's advice without doing your analysis, and it results in a loss. In both cases, you're not trading based on your conviction but on the opinions of others. This can lead to inconsistent decision-making and poor results.

To become a confident and independent trader, you need to stop seeking validation and start trusting yourself. This doesn't mean ignoring advice from experienced traders or mentors, but it means taking responsibility for your own decisions. **Instead of asking others what they think of your trades, focus on improving your analysis skills**. Learn to trust your strategy and follow your trading plan, even if others don't agree with your approach.

One way to build confidence is by keeping a trading journal. After each trade, write down why you made the trade, what went well, and what didn't. Over time, you'll start to see patterns in your decision-making process, and you'll be able to identify areas where you can improve. This self-reflection will help you become more confident in your abilities, and you'll stop feeling the need to seek validation from others.

Another important point is that everyone's trading style is different. What works for one person may not work for another. Just because someone else is successful with a particular strategy doesn't mean it will suit you. By focusing on your research and learning from your experiences, you can develop a trading style that fits your personality, risk tolerance, and goals.

In conclusion, seeking validation from others can hold you back as a trader. It's natural to want reassurance, especially when you're new to trading, but relying on others for approval can weaken your confidence and lead to poor decision-making. The most successful traders are those who trust their research and take full responsibility for their trades. By focusing on improving your skills and learning from your mistakes, you can become a confident and independent trader who doesn't need external validation.

Examples :

In derivative trading, quick and accurate decision-making is crucial. However, seeking validation can lead to delays and confusion, costing traders valuable opportunities. Let me share the story of Mr. Sharma, a positional trader who experienced this firsthand.

On October 26, 2023, Mr Sharma's technical analysis indicated that the market was in an oversold zone, suggesting it was a good time to buy. Moreover, he noticed that foreign institutional investors (FIIs) had taken aggressive short positions, accounting for almost 90% of their activity in the derivative market. His data analysis hinted that the FIIs might soon cover their shorts, which could lead to a sharp market bounce. Everything pointed to a buying opportunity.

However, instead of acting on his insights, Mr. Sharma hesitated. He sought validation from fundamental factors, which looked daunting due to the ongoing conflict in Israel. His fear of making the wrong move kept him from taking action. As a result, he missed a significant buying opportunity when the market did indeed bounce back sharply. This experience taught him that relying too much on external validation can hinder his trading success. Sometimes, trusting your analysis is the best way forward.

21. Stay in the Game

In trading, there's a saying: "The most important rule is to stay in the game." What this means is that your survival as a trader is more important than any single win or loss. Trading is a long-term journey, and your primary goal should be to preserve your capital so that you can continue to trade and learn over time. Many traders, especially beginners, get so focused on chasing profits that they forget the importance of protecting their accounts from major losses. But without capital, you can't trade—and without trading, you can't succeed.

Let's start by understanding why staying in the game is so important. The stock market is unpredictable. No matter how skilled or experienced you are, there will be times when the market goes against you. It's easy to get caught up in the excitement of trying to make quick profits, but if you take on too much risk, a single bad trade can wipe out a significant portion of your account. That's why it's crucial to always think about the long-term game and prioritize survival over short-term gains.

One of the key ways to stay in the game is through risk management. This means setting limits on how much you're willing to lose on any given trade. **A common rule of thumb is to never risk more than 1-2% of your total account on a single trade.** This way, even if a trade goes against you, it won't have a major impact on your overall capital. By managing your risk carefully, you ensure that a few bad trades won't knock you out of the market.

Another aspect of staying in the game is taking care of your mental health. Trading can be emotionally exhausting, especially during periods of high volatility or after a string of losses. It's important to recognize when you need to take a break. If you find yourself feeling overwhelmed, frustrated, or overly emotional, it might be time to step away from the market for a while. Taking breaks helps you clear your mind, reduce stress, and come back with a fresh perspective. Remember, your mental well-being is just as important as your capital when it comes to long-term success in trading.

It's also essential to keep learning and adapting. The market is constantly changing, and strategies that work today might not be effective tomorrow. **Staying in the game means being open to learning new techniques, studying market trends, and continuously improving your skills.** Successful traders are those who are flexible and willing to adapt to new market conditions. By staying informed and always looking for ways to improve, you'll increase your chances of long-term success.

In addition to preserving your capital and mental health, staying in the game also means having realistic expectations. Trading is not a get-rich-quick scheme, and it's important to be patient. Many traders quit after a few losses because they expected instant success. However, the reality is that trading is a skill that takes time to develop. It's better to focus on steady, consistent growth rather than trying to hit big home runs with every trade.

In conclusion, staying in the game is the most important rule of trading. Your long-term success depends on your ability to manage risk, protect your capital, and maintain a healthy mindset. By focusing on survival rather than short-term profits, you'll allow yourself to learn, grow, and succeed in the market over time. **Trading is a marathon, not a sprint, and those who stay in the game are the ones who ultimately achieve lasting success.**

Example :

Staying in the game is crucial, especially when it comes to risk management. Many investors tend to overlook this during a bull market, leading to significant losses. Let me tell you about my family friend, Aditi, who fell victim to poor risk management.

In 2023, Aditi was a rational trader with an impressive track record; her predictions were right 90% of the time. She initially used ₹3 crores as her trading capital, but her success led her to increase it dramatically to ₹50 crores, thinking her winning streak would continue. However, as the market shifted, her success ratio fell to 50%. In 2024, she faced a staggering loss of ₹5 crores.

Unable to tolerate such a significant setback, Aditi decided to quit trading altogether. This experience highlights the importance of sticking to risk management principles, no matter how confident you feel. Remember, it's essential to stay in the game to ride out the inevitable ups and downs of trading.

Quality that Traders develop eventually

<u>A)Discipline</u>

Discipline in trading is like following a strict diet or workout plan. When you set up a trading strategy, you create a clear plan with specific rules for when to buy and sell stocks. This plan helps you avoid making random decisions based on emotions or market noise. Sticking to this plan is crucial for success.

In the world of trading, it's easy to get swayed by market trends or the latest news. For example, if you hear that a stock is about to rise because of a new product launch, you might be tempted to buy it without checking if it fits your trading strategy. However, if you follow your plan, you'll avoid making impulsive trades based on rumours or excitement.

Over time, consistently following your trading strategy builds discipline. You learn to make decisions based on your research and rules, not on how you feel at the moment. **This discipline is not only useful in trading but also transfers to other areas of your life. For instance, if you set goals for your personal life or career, sticking to a structured plan becomes easier. Whether you're trying to save money, complete a project, or adopt a healthy lifestyle, the**

discipline you develop from trading helps you stay focused and committed.

In trading, discipline also means not letting losses or gains affect your decision-making. If a trade goes against you, sticking to your plan and accepting the loss calmly is part of the discipline. Similarly, after a big win, staying grounded and continuing to follow your rules without becoming overly confident is crucial. This balanced approach helps you avoid making emotional decisions, which can lead to mistakes.

The discipline you develop as a trader helps you create a structured approach to problems. Instead of reacting impulsively, you start to analyze situations more carefully, set clear goals, and follow a plan to achieve them. This structured thinking helps in managing time effectively, prioritizing tasks, and making informed decisions in various aspects of life.

In summary, discipline is one of the most valuable traits developed through trading. It teaches you to stick to your rules and follow a structured approach, which benefits not only your trading performance but also your personal and professional life. The habits of planning, consistency, and emotional control you develop through trading can greatly enhance your overall discipline.

<u>B)Patience</u>

Patience is a critical quality in trading and can have a significant impact on your life. In trading, you need to wait for the right setup before entering a trade. This means you don't just jump into trades based on gut feelings or short-term market movements. Instead, you wait for the market to present a clear opportunity that fits your strategy.

For example, if you are waiting for a stock to reach a certain price before buying, you need to exercise patience. The stock might fluctuate up and down, but you stick to your plan and wait for the right moment. This patience helps you avoid making hasty decisions that can lead to losses. It also teaches you to analyze situations carefully and wait for the best possible outcome.

In life, patience helps you handle delays and challenges more effectively. Whether you're working on a long-term project, waiting for a promotion, or dealing with personal issues, the ability to stay calm and wait for the right time can make a big difference. Instead of becoming frustrated or giving up, you learn to approach challenges with a steady mindset and keep working towards your goals.

Patience also helps in managing expectations. In trading, you know that not every trade will be a winner and that there will be periods of losses or stagnation. Accepting this and not getting discouraged is part of being patient. This mindset helps you remain positive and focused on long-term success, rather than getting bogged down by short-term setbacks.

Furthermore, patience in trading teaches you to make well-considered decisions rather than acting impulsively. This quality is valuable in everyday life, where making thoughtful decisions can lead to better outcomes. For instance, when faced with a difficult decision, taking the time to weigh your options and consider the consequences helps you make more informed choices.

In summary, patience is a vital quality developed through trading. It helps you wait for the right opportunities, handle delays and challenges calmly, and make thoughtful decisions. The patience you cultivate in trading benefits various aspects of your life, making you more resilient and focused on achieving your goals.

C)Emotional Control

Emotional control is essential in trading and can greatly influence your overall well-being. The stock market is full of ups and downs, and learning to manage your emotions is key to making rational decisions. In trading, you'll encounter moments of excitement, fear, greed, and frustration. How you handle these emotions can determine your success.

For example, if a trade is going well, it's easy to get greedy and hold on for too long, hoping for even higher gains. Conversely, if a trade is going poorly, you might feel anxious or fearful, leading you to sell hastily to avoid further losses. Learning to control these emotions helps you stick to your trading plan and make decisions based on logic rather than feelings.

Emotional control also helps you handle stress more effectively. Trading can be stressful, especially during periods of high volatility or after experiencing losses. **Developing the ability to stay calm and focused, regardless of market conditions, improves your overall stress management. This skill is valuable in everyday life, where maintaining composure during challenging situations helps you make better decisions and handle difficulties more effectively.**

Additionally, controlling your emotions in trading leads to better decision-making. When you let emotions drive your actions, you're more likely to make impulsive or irrational decisions. By learning to manage your emotions, you ensure that your decisions are based on analysis and strategy, rather than knee-jerk reactions.

This emotional control translates into better relationships and interactions in your personal life. Being able to manage your emotions helps you communicate more effectively, resolve conflicts calmly, and make thoughtful decisions. It also reduces the impact of stress and frustration on your overall well-being, leading to a more balanced and harmonious life.

In conclusion, emotional control is a crucial skill developed through trading. It helps you manage stress, make rational decisions, and maintain composure during challenging times. The ability to control your emotions benefits various aspects of life, improving your overall well-being and interpersonal relationships.

D)Resilience

Resilience is like having the ability to bounce back after a tough situation, and it is a vital skill for successful trading. In the stock market, losses are inevitable. No matter how well you plan or how skilled you are, you will face setbacks. Learning how to deal with these losses without letting them affect your confidence or motivation is what builds resilience.

Imagine you have invested in a stock expecting it to rise, but instead, it falls. Initially, this can be disappointing and frustrating. You might feel like giving up or questioning your abilities. However, resilience means you don't let a single loss define you or derail your trading journey. Instead, you use it as a learning opportunity. You analyze what went wrong, adjust your strategy if needed, and continue forward with a positive mindset.

In trading, resilience helps you maintain your mental toughness. It's not just about recovering from financial losses but also about dealing with the emotional impact. Trading can be stressful, especially when you face a series of losses. A resilient trader is someone who can handle these ups and downs without becoming disheartened or losing focus.

Developing resilience through trading is beneficial in many areas of life. For instance, in your personal life or career, you will encounter challenges and failures. Whether you're facing a setback at work or a personal issue, the ability to bounce back with determination is crucial.

Resilience helps you stay motivated and continue working towards your goals despite obstacles.

Resilience also involves learning from mistakes. Each loss in trading provides valuable lessons. By analyzing what went wrong and how you can improve, you build a stronger strategy and become better at managing risks. This approach of learning from failures and continuously improving is essential not just in trading but in any field.

Moreover, resilience helps you maintain a long-term perspective. In trading, focusing only on short-term results can lead to frustration and poor decisions. Instead, a resilient trader understands that success comes from sticking to a well-thought-out plan and being patient. This long-term perspective is equally important in personal and professional life, where consistent effort and perseverance lead to success.

In summary, resilience is a critical quality developed through trading. It helps you deal with losses, maintain motivation, and continue improving despite setbacks. This mental toughness is valuable in all areas of life, enabling you to overcome challenges and keep working towards your goals with confidence and determination.

5. Critical Thinking

Critical thinking is the ability to analyze situations, make informed decisions, and solve problems logically. In trading, this skill is essential because it involves examining market trends, data, and news to make sound investment choices. By developing critical thinking through trading, you enhance your ability to assess various situations and make well-thought-out decisions in everyday life.

When you trade, you don't just act on instinct. Instead, you gather and analyze data such as stock prices, financial reports, and market news. For instance, if you are considering investing in a company, you would look at its financial health, industry trends, and any recent news that might affect its performance. This process of evaluating all relevant information and considering different factors before making a decision is a key aspect of critical thinking.

Critical thinking helps you weigh the pros and cons of different options. In trading, you might face multiple investment opportunities and need to choose the best one. By critically analyzing each option's potential risks and rewards, you make informed decisions that align with your trading goals. This approach reduces the likelihood of making impulsive or emotional trades that can lead to losses.

In everyday life, critical thinking enhances your problem-solving abilities. Whether you're making a major purchase, planning a project, or resolving a conflict, the ability to analyze information, consider different perspectives, and evaluate

outcomes helps you make better decisions. For example, if you're deciding between two job offers, critical thinking allows you to assess factors like salary, career growth, and work-life balance to choose the best option.

Moreover, critical thinking improves your ability to anticipate potential challenges and develop strategies to address them. In trading, this means being prepared for market fluctuations and having a plan in place to manage risks. In your personal and professional life, this skill helps you foresee potential problems and create effective solutions.

Additionally, critical thinking fosters a more analytical mindset. Instead of accepting information at face value, you learn to question and verify it. This habit of questioning and seeking evidence improves your decision-making and helps you avoid misinformation or biased opinions.

In conclusion, critical thinking is a crucial skill developed through trading that enhances your ability to make informed decisions, solve problems, and evaluate options. This skill is valuable in all aspects of life, helping you approach challenges with a logical and analytical mindset. By developing critical thinking through trading, you improve your overall decision-making abilities and become more adept at handling various situations effectively.

May I ask you for a small favour?

I want to thank you for reading this book at the outset. You could have chosen any book, but you took mine, and I appreciate this.

I hope you got at least some information and that you enjoyed reading this book.

Can I ask for 30 seconds more of your time?

I'd love it if you could leave a review of the book. Reviews may not matter to big-name authors, but they're a tremendous help for authors like me, who don't have much following. They help me to grow my readership by encouraging folks to take a chance on my books.

In simple words - reviews are the lifeblood of any author.

Please leave your review of the book.

It will take less than a minute of your time and tremendously help me reach out to more people, so please leave your review.

Thanks for your support of my work. And I'd love to see your review.

www.ingramcontent.com/pod-product-compliance
Lightning Source LLC
Chambersburg PA
CBHW031634170726
47990CB00017B/1014